So You Want to *Marry* My Daughter?

Paul Friesen combines the wisdom and humor from family counseling, personal experience, and raising three daughters to develop this must-read guide for all young men and dads with daughters. His insightful questions led me to re-examine my relationship with my daughter, and provided guidance to help with the raising of my two sons. I highly recommend it for all males from 13 to 80.

John Eunice III, Colonel, United States Air Force

With such few words, Paul Friesen captures the importance of one of the most dramatic moments in parents' lives. He does it with real spiritual insight, great common sense, and delightful humor. This little book should be on the front steps of every Christian marriage proposal!

Dr. David Horn, Director of the Ockenga Institute
Gordon-Conwell Theological Seminary, S. Hamilton, Massachusetts

Paul and Virginia Friesen have been our friends for over thirty years. They have raised three wonderful daughters. Paul's book is full of common sense questions to ask any young man who wishes to date your daughter. It is a guide you can refer to over and over. We all want the best for our children and this will help.

Bob and Carol Kraning

As a father of two incredible daughters, I have often shuddered to think that some guy would come waltzing into their lives, sweeping them off their feet and out of my world. Now, thanks to Paul Friesen, we fathers have some pro-active ammunition. My first time through *So You Want to Marry My Daughter?* left me laughing at Paul's humor, wit, and wisdom. My second reading moved me to thank the Lord for Paul's insight and genuinely Biblical counsel. Buy one for each of your kids. It will help your daughter recognize a good man, and help your son become one.

David W. Hegg, Pastor/Teacher
Northpoint Evangelical Free Church, Corona, California

In an age where relationships are self-serving and marriages are conditional, Paul gives us Biblical wisdom on the front end to lay the foundation for a successful marriage. As a father of three future brides, this read is an exceptional filter for all who dare grace the door.

Grant Williams, 10-year NFL veteran
Superbowl XXXVI Champion, New England Patriots

So You Want to Marry My Daughter? is a must-read for every father of daughters, and a strongly-suggested read for every young man contemplating engagement. Dr. Friesen has been there, having given permission for a young man to marry his daughter Kari, and in this book he offers both spiritual and practical wisdom on how to think about this decision that most fathers of daughters will face. Unfortunately, most fathers today don't take their role in this transition seriously enough, feeling I suppose that the decision to marry has already been made and that they can only give permission (or not) at the end of the process. Dr. Friesen reminds us that fathers need to take an active role and have a strong voice in their daughters' relationships and to help everyone involved think rightly about engagement and marriage. In this short, readable book, Dr. Friesen frames 10 simple questions, the answers to which get at the heart of what a father needs to hear from a prospective son-in-law. Get it; read it; use it. I plan on giving it to all my friends who have daughters, as well as to my son (who may get married sooner than I imagine).

Rev. Erich Becker, Director of HomeFront
Grace Fellowship Church, Timonium, Maryland

While we have all laughed at the old saying that "no one is good enough for my daughter," when it actually *is* your daughter, it doesn't sound so quaint. After loving and providing for her for 20 or 25 years, to have some young man waltz into her life and ask to take her away is a frightening and sometimes sickening thought. Who is he? What is he really like? There is so much I want to know about him but don't even know what questions to ask!

Well, here is the help we have been looking for. In *So You Want to Marry My Daughter?*, Paul Friesen offers fathers and prospective grooms the tools with which to evaluate the proposed marriage, to get to know one another, and to forge a relationship that will promote a bond of respect and love between the two most important men in your little girl's life. The material is Biblical, practical, and written for men . . . an easy read.

Rev. Howard Clark

Most men agree that having our children in "God honoring marriages" would be a touchdown! From the time the nurse in the delivery room hands them off in that tight, little bundle we just try not to fumble. Dr. Friesen's earlier book, *Letters to my Daughters*, is perfect for the play-calling offensive coordinator. But late in the game, with a culture that is blitzing on every down, *So You Want to Marry my Daughter?* will get you to pay dirt!

Dave Sherman, Kaylee and Whitnee's dad

So You Want to Marry My Daughter?

The top 10 questions every dad should ask and every young man should be prepared to answer before engagement (way before!)

Dr. Paul A. Friesen

Home Improvement Ministries
Bedford, Massachusetts

So You Want to Marry My Daughter?

Cover photography by Ruettgers Photography www.ruettgers.com
Design and production: Barbara Steele
Copy editing: Guy Steele

ISBN-10: 0-9789931-1-X
ISBN-13: 978-0-9789931-1-5

Published by HOME IMPROVEMENT MINISTRIES.
For information on other H.I.M. resources, please contact:
HOME IMPROVEMENT MINISTRIES, 209 Burlington Road, Bedford, MA 01730.
E-mail inquiries: info@HIMweb.org
Website: www.HIMweb.org

Unless otherwise noted, all scripture quotations are from the HOLY BIBLE: NEW INTERNATIONAL VERSION. Copyright © 1973, 1978, 1984 by the International Bible Society.

Printed in the United States of America.   9/6-07TPS/4K

Dedication

To Kari and Gabe

Kari, thanks for pursuing God in your life
and for choosing such a Godly man.

Gabe, thanks for intentionally choosing
to grow in Christlikeness
and for loving our daughter so well.

Contents

Foreword
by Gabriel Garcia

So you want to marry my daughter? Actually, *I* wanted to marry *his* daughter.

In my life, there hasn't been a more daunting task than trying to build up the courage to ask Paul Friesen if he would give me his permission to marry his eldest daughter Kari. This isn't a conversation that one has every day, so there were some obvious nerves involved. After dating and falling in love with Kari over the course of a couple of years, I finally realized that I would be crazy not to spend the rest of my life with this amazing woman. To make that leap, I first had to receive Paul's blessing to move forward with the engagement.

To be honest, I had grand thoughts about skipping the whole idea of asking for permission. I am so thankful that I pushed through my fears to have this sacred conversation with the father of the woman that I would soon marry. I greatly appreciated that Paul was willing to ask tough and penetrating questions about my relationship with Kari and about our plans for the future. Though I may not have had all the "right" answers, I know Paul appreciated my honesty and my sincere heart. By answering each of the questions that he had prepared, I also became more confident that I was making one of the best decisions of my life.

So You Want to Marry My Daughter? is a book I wish Paul had written *before* I wanted to marry his daughter.

11

This fun and challenging book is full of Biblical principles that should serve as a great resource both to fathers and to men contemplating marriage. For those fathers who have been given the assignment of raising daughters, this book can help you to have confidence that you are handing her off to a Godly man who will love and serve her throughout her life. I truly believe that asking me each of the questions found in this book was one of the greatest ways Paul showed his love for Kari. Any man considering marriage should read this book and examine whether or not he is willing to make the sacrifices that are needed to lead and love his future wife in a way that brings honor to God.

Paul Friesen is one of the godliest men in my life. He has modeled to me what it means to be a great husband and father through his servant leadership. A great testament to his life and ministry is that he has three daughters (and now a son-in-law) who have authentic and passionate relationships with the Lord.

I am confident that you will thoroughly enjoy this book while being equipped to ask—or answer—ten of the most important questions that serve as the foundation to any marriage.

Blessings,
Gabriel Garcia
Roseville, California
July 2007

Foreword
by Jim Burns, Ph.D.

When Paul Friesen speaks, I listen. When Paul Friesen writes, I read. He and his wonderful wife, Virginia, definitely know what they are talking about, because they have lived it out with their own family. They have also influenced the lives of thousands of people with God-honoring and life-changing messages for their families and their marriages. This book is actually about legacy building. The purpose of people like the Friesens is to mentor us as parents. We then mentor our children, and the legacy of faith continues to the next generation.

Paul had no idea how important and personal this book would become for me. The week he sent me the manuscript of *So You Want to Marry My Daughter?*, my own daughter became engaged. A few weeks before, Dave, who had moved from "just another boy" to "the *one* and only," had asked me for permission to marry our daughter. I have read every word of this manuscript and underlined half the book. The book is Paul at his best: practical, spiritually challenging, and fun to read.

Besides your daughter's decision to be committed to Jesus Christ, there is no more important relationship than to the one she will choose to marry. Your daughter is moving from dependence on you, toward independence. She is doing what the Bible strongly charges us to do and that is leave her father and mother and be united with her spouse.

Far too many parents don't take the time to mentor their daughters or their sons in this, the second most important decision of their child's life. I hope you get as much out of this book as I did. Some of the questions are hard to ask and some are just plain good advice. I strongly urge you to help prepare your daughter and her special someone to make the right decisions. What a privilege to have Paul Friesen's wisdom and counsel on this journey, as you delicately look at these most important questions. Happy reading and communicating.

Jim Burns, Ph.D.
President, HomeWord
Author of *Creating an Intimate Marriage* and *Confident Parenting*

Acknowledgments

This book originated, though not in written form, long before August 1, 2006, when Gabe asked for Kari's hand in marriage. The material for this book started when our daughters were born and I began thinking about a day when another man would take them away from me. So, I want to first acknowledge my love and appreciation to Kari, Lisa, and Julie, daughters who have caused me to ponder how best to assist them in the process of entering into a life-long relationship with another man; and to Gabe, a man who loves God and has honored us as Kari's parents. You have each brought me more joy than I deserve or ever imagined.

Second, I want to express my appreciation to my parents, though no longer living, for modeling to their four daughters and a son how good it is to love the Lord fully and marry like-minded mates.

Third, I want to express my deep gratitude to Frank and Esther Collins for raising such an incredible daughter who was worth the "risk" of asking permission to marry. Thanks for saying yes to my request on December 15, 1975, and for entrusting your precious daughter to me. You have been wonderful parents-in-law, and I thank God for you.

Fourth, without the Home Improvement Ministries board, this book and the ministry we are enjoying would not have been a reality. Thank you for your encouragement, advice, and sacrifice on our behalf.

Fifth, special thanks to Erich and Ginny Becker, Seth Bilazarian, Jim Burns, Howard Clark, John Eunice, Ellen Gabrielse, Gary Gaddini, Gabriel Garcia, Richard and Kit Hendricks, Rick Hendricks, David Horn, Ray Johnston, Bob Kraning, Dan Robbins, Scott Shaull, David Sherman, Carter and Tracy Welch, Rick Welles, and Grant Williams, who all read and gave helpful feedback on the manuscript.

Sixth, "thanks" is an inadequate word to express my deep appreciation for Barbara and Guy Steele, our long-time friends and partners in ministry. Your countless hours, incredible expertise, and creativity in design and editing have been gifts I can never repay.

Seventh, though my name is listed as the author, this is a book that comes out of 31 years of partnering in parenting and marriage with the most gifted and talented woman, mother, and wife I can imagine. Thank you, Virginia, for saying yes to me over 31 years ago and being the woman I am so thankful I asked permission to marry. I love you.

Finally, if any good is received from this book, it will be because of the work of the Holy Spirit moving in the hearts and lives of the readers. I am humbled to be part of God's family and to be given the privilege to pen these words. May all the glory go to You, heavenly Father, and may the lives of the men who read these pages become more conformed to the image of your Son.

So You Want to Marry My Daughter?

The day *Father of the Bride* went from a comedy movie to a reality show

On August 1, 2006, the Steve Martin film *Father of the Bride*, one of my favorite movies, became a reality show rather than a comedy when Gabriel Steven Garcia asked for the hand of my eldest daughter, Kari, in marriage. For some, the real-life version of *Father of the Bride* may be a drama, while for others it may, unfortunately, seem more like a tragedy. For all of us as dads, it is the day we realize that our little girl has grown up and we will soon be giving her to another man. Our days of being her provider and protector are coming to an end. We may still be "Dad" and she may still be our daughter, but we are no longer to be the number one man in her life, the man she turns to for answers, and the one who is her primary adviser and confidante.

As part of God's plan, our daughters are to "leave" us and be united to another man. The two of them are to become one (something fathers and daughters, no matter how close, were never designed to be). Daughters are given to us as gifts to be cared for, for a season, and then to be given away to another.

But before we give our precious daughter away to this young man, we have the privilege and responsibility of giving some input on this huge decision our daughter is about to make. About a half hour into my conversation with Gabe, I said, "I bet you were hoping for a simple 'yes' or 'no' to your question." Before we give that simple "yes" or "no" it is our responsibility, to the best of our knowledge, to try to discern if this man is really going to be to our daughter all that he is expected to be according to scripture. Is he going to love her, cherish her, care for her, provide for her, lead her, and be her covenant partner as long as he lives?

In the next pages I am going to pose a few questions I think every father has the right—no, the responsibility—to ask of the man to whom he is giving his daughter, *before* saying yes or no. This is, undoubtedly, a decision that will affect the rest of her life more than any other decision. A daughter may have made mistakes along the way. She may have cheated in high school, gotten drunk at a party, had sex with some guy she hardly knew, or become pregnant. But this decision is for life. We're talking about the guy she intends to be with for the rest of her life. This decision, whether right or wrong, will affect her, us, and our grandchildren more than one can imagine.

If you are a son, these questions would be good ones to brush up on. Not like cramming to know the "right" answers (though Gabe feels the future suitors of our other two daughters will have an advantage he didn't have—they will be taking an open-book quiz, whereas he had to go in without any advance warning). As a son, you are called to live life intentionally so that you are prepared to answer these questions with integrity and confidence.

I hope you laugh a lot while reading these pages, ponder some, and ask God for wisdom often. This is a book written for men in a way I trust men will take the time to read—even if it's just the bullets. Hey, the print is big, the spacing generous; there are cartoons, and you can get credit for reading a book. Happy reading!

The Questions

"Why do you want to marry my daughter?"

Answers you don't want to hear:

- Because she is hot.
- I need someone to put me through school.
- My folks kicked me out of their house.
- I really want to try married sex.
- My parole officer said it would be good for me to marry.

Answers you do want to hear:

- Your daughter is amazing.
- I am so thankful God brought her into my life.
- I feel the two of us working together can accomplish much for the Kingdom.
- She is incredibly special, and I want to serve her and care for her the rest of her life.
- I believe we encourage each other to become what God intends us to be.

Critical concepts you need to hear:

- He sees her as an incredible woman, a true gift of God to him.
- They encourage each other to be more Christ-like.
- He wants to serve her and meet her needs as much as any human is able.

For those who want more:

Every dad wants someone to love his daughter and care for her after he is gone. We want someone who will not only provide for her physically but care for her emotionally and encourage her spiritually to become all she can be. We want every assurance that our daughter is marrying a man of character and integrity. The best way to see what he will likely be in the future is to try to see as much as possible who he has been in the past.

Take initiative to spend time with him. Invite him over for meals, events, and even vacations. You want to give him time to be with you in a variety of situations. He needs to get to know you as well, as this will be part of his decision-making process regarding your daughter, so don't mess it up.

When you ask, "Why do you want to marry my daughter?" the answer, "Because I love her," may sound good, but it is of little comfort. He likely has told many girls that he loved them over the course of his dating life. You want to see character more than charisma at this point.

You want your daughter's prospective husband to feel that he is "marrying up," and that he is fortunate to have found a woman like this. You want him to be amazed that she is in love with him. You want to observe that he treats her like a princess. If he is not considerate of her now and doesn't put her needs ahead of his own, he likely will not do so after marriage. You want to be hearing from your daughter about how well he is treating her, rather than hearing excuses from your daughter such as "He was tired," "He is shy," or "He may be explosive, but he cools down quickly."

We want a man who encourages our daughter to grow in her relationship with Christ. Is she growing more spiritually mature because of this relationship, or is she the one who seems to constantly try to pull *him* up? Seeing that he takes initiative to seek out ways they can grow through times together, exposure to other couples, and teaching experiences, is important.

"Mr. and Mrs. Ackerman, I'll come to the point. I'm deeply in love with your daughter, and I'd like to move in with you."

To be honest, most of us married our wives so our needs could be met. Such thinking may be natural, but it puts a great deal of pressure on a wife. We want a son-in-law who pretty much "had it together" *before* he met our daughter. He need not be perfect, of course, but neither should he be a candidate for "extreme makeover." The mystery of marriage is that two wholes become one, not two halves. Certainly both husband and wife are to meet each other's needs—but sad indeed is the marriage in which the husband believes the woman was put in his life exclusively to meet his needs. If a man considers it is his wife's duty to meet all his needs, he will forever be frustrated that she is falling short. But if he believes he and his wife were given to each other to meet each other's needs, then they will always have ample opportunity to do that very thing.

Bottom line:

- Are you hearing that he thinks she is wonderful?
- Are you hearing that he wants to serve her?
- Are you hearing that he feels they help each other to grow spiritually?

"What are you doing to prepare for and confirm the marriage decision?"

Answers you don't want to hear:

- I don't care what all her friends say, I am not a jerk.
- It doesn't matter what our families say, it's *our* life.
- It doesn't make any sense to me either, but I guess that's love.
- Prepare? I didn't prepare to be a garbage collector and now I are one.
- My parole officer said I better make better decisions in the future or I'll land back in jail.

Answers you do want to hear:

- So far, all our family members have given us their approval.
- We have hung out a lot with those who know us best, so they could give us their input.
- Both my mentor and hers have been very affirming regarding our relationship.
- We have read 5 books our pastor gave us to help us

think through and prepare for this decision.

- We have attended a "pre-engagement" seminar and plan to have specific pre-marital counseling to help us think through areas we may not have dealt with.

Critical concepts you need to hear:

- They are getting counsel from those who know them best.
- They are not isolating themselves.
- They are receiving input through books and classes.

For those who want more:

To make a sports team, you study the plays, follow the conditioning plan, and try out to make the team. To be in a theatrical performance, you take drama classes, study the script, ask others to coach you, and then audition to see if you're a good "fit" for the cast. But to get married, you get a marriage license, have just about anyone perform the ceremony, and you're married.

We conduct a number of engagement and pre-engagement weekends each year. One of the questions on the "pre-session questionnaire" asks the couples who are planning to attend the weekend to rate the response of their family, friends, pastor, etc., on a scale of 1 to 10, 1 being totally against the marriage and 10 being totally for the marriage. The response on one woman's questionnaire had a 1 from parents, siblings, and best friends. She went ahead and married against all their misgivings. Three weeks after they were married, she filed for divorce. What was she thinking? *Was* she thinking? As they say, love is blind, but marriage is a real eye opener. I can't emphasize enough the importance of the couple listening closely to those who know them best and are willing to be honest. It is critical that the friends giving input are friends who have a history of speaking truth, even if it is not well received.

We counseled a couple that had both come out of divorces and each had children. The children had huge reservations about the upcoming marriage, as did many close friends. Most of the friends, however, did not speak up because they were afraid of "losing the friendship." But one brave friend wrote a very respectful letter expressing all her reservations.

"You want only happiness, Douglas. I want wealth, power, fame, and happiness."

She wrote in the letter, "I know this may cost us our friendship, but I love you too much to remain silent." Oh, that all couples had such friends!

Another critical area you want to make sure you are hearing regards who or what situations are helping your daughter and her future spouse to prepare intentionally, not just for the wedding, but also for a life of marriage together.

We were at the Mount Washington Hotel in New Hampshire one October and noticed a huge tent set up outside. We asked one of the staff members about it. "Oh, it was for a wedding we did here yesterday. The cost from the hotel alone was $250,000 for the 250 guests." I couldn't help but wonder how much money and time had gone into preparing for their marriage. On a scale more of us are familiar with, I am oftentimes a bit amused (and dismayed) to be part of a wedding where the couple "could not afford" premarital counseling or classes, and yet a guy in a tux standing by a stretch limo was getting more than what it would have cost to pay for some great marriage preparation.

For those who truly can not afford it, or do not have access to pre-marital counseling, I would make sure the couple is doing some very intentional reading. There are a number of great resources out there today. One of the best is a sixteen-week series of studies for couples called *Preparing for Marriage*, edited by Dennis Rainey. It is very thorough and is 251 pages long. I have given out hundreds of copies and yet few have finished it. Couples say, "It takes too long." Might I suggest that time and money spent in counseling and preparation *before* the marriage, rather than in counseling *after* the marriage, are time and money well spent.

As we tell our couples at our engagement weekends, there will be one of three results from this weekend: a confirmation that you are right for each other; a realization that there are areas that need additional work before you are ready to decide on marriage; or an acknowledgement that you are not right for each other. Any of these three could be considered a "good" result.

Encourage your daughter and prospective son-in-law to take their time. Time only confirms. We suggest the "four season rule": a couple should take at least a year to get to know each other *before* considering marriage so they are more able to see each other in all seasons and occasions and have enough time for family and friends to truly get to know them in a variety of situations.

Bottom Line:

- Is there confirmation from family and friends?
- Are they getting professional objective input?
- Are they taking enough time to process others' input?

"What are your passions in life and how do you plan to encourage those of my daughter?"

Answers you don't want to hear:

- I really just take it a day at a time.
- I'm really into video games.
- Why does she need passions?
- Women have spiritual gifts?
- My parole officer said it was my passions that landed me in jail!

Answers you do want to hear:

- I am so thankful for the support she gives to me, but I want to make sure her desires don't get lost.
- I really have a passion for helping the homeless.
- I love working with junior high kids; whether formally or informally, I expect to work with youth.
- God has gifted her in remarkable ways. I want to encourage her to develop her gifts fully.
- I seem to be gifted in business and helping others succeed.

Critical concepts you need to hear:

- There is something that makes him come alive.
- He takes delight in her accomplishments and passions and has a deep desire to help her realize her dreams.
- His passions are not in conflict with what you know your daughter's to be.

For those who want more:

In the book *Wild at Heart*, John Eldredge says, "Don't ask yourself what the world needs. Ask yourself what makes you come alive, and go do that, because what the world needs is people who have come alive."[1] In my observation, we are living in a time when many young men lack passion and direction in life. We dads need to ask about this—not just "Do you have a job?" but "What is it that really drives you and motivates you? What is it you dream about when you wake up, as you are going to sleep, or when you are driving alone in the car? Are you thinking about the next time you can surf, eat, get to your couch to watch TV, or play the newest video game? Are you thinking about sex, making money, or buying a new car? What is it that gives your life meaning? What do you love most?"

We want to know that our daughter is marrying a man who currently has passions, and that they are legal, moral, and productive. All my girls have had a passion for ministry from the teen years of their lives on. Those passions have

---

1. Eldredge, J. (2001). *Wild at Heart* (p. 200). Nashville, TN: Thomas Nelson, Inc.

been expressed differently: one works in youth ministry, one is an athletic trainer, and one is an athlete. I am not worried about whether or not those passions will change in the specific application because I know their deepest passion is to serve Christ. I also know that those who have passions and follow them usually have the character to achieve whatever they are passionate about.

It is possible to see those passions in someone before marriage. You don't need to hang around someone for very long to see if he is motivated and passionate about life. Too many marriages suffer because the husband just works to live—and lives for nothing. You want to see someone who dreams, who has something that gets him up in the morning or keeps him awake at night. You want a man who is passionate about making a difference for eternity, whatever his vocation ends up being.

"*For the time being we'll be living with my folks, but our ultimate goal is to live with Denise's folks.*"

In *Don't Waste Your Life*, John Piper recounts an article from the *Reader's Digest* describing a couple who " 'took early retirement from their jobs in the Northeast five years ago when he was 59 and she was 51. Now they live in Punta Gorda, Florida, where they cruise on their 30-foot trawler, play softball, and collect shells. . . .' Picture them before Christ at the great day of judgment: 'Look, Lord. See my shells.' That is a tragedy."[2]

I realize that the decisions and passions of the man marrying my daughter will determine to a great extent what they experience as a couple in life and what they will some day reflect about as they look back on life. When that time comes, many years from now, I wish for them much more than sea shells.

In addition to a man who has clear passions of his own, I long for a man who is able to encourage the passions of my daughter as well. One of the delights of being a dad is seeing and helping your "little girl" grow up to be a woman with gifts and passions of her own. As a dad, you take delight in attending sporting events, paying for music lessons, taking her to drama practice, and buying her favorite books. As she grows older, you see her passions and gifts become more focused. You long for her to marry a man who will take over your role as primary cheerleader—not that you will no longer give her encouragement, but you are no longer to be her primary confidante, adviser, and fan.

Though we supposedly live in an "advanced culture" that does not believe in gender superiority, far too many men still expect their wives to shelve their own gifts, passions, and

2. Piper, J. (2003). *Don't Waste Your Life*. Crossway Books.

abilities and focus solely on making their husbands comfortable and successful.

In many cases, the husband's career is on a steep incline just as the wife starts to bear children. I believe nurturing children is the highest calling a mother has, and in no way do I want to imply she should "leave" home to pursue her other passions. Children need both mom and dad as much as possible and careers should never take precedence over parenting. With that said, however, husbands should be committed to helping their wives continue to develop their gifts and passions. It could be a writing class she is interested in taking, or a Bible study she wants to be part of, or a physical fitness routine that is important to her. You want a man for your daughter who will appreciate her talents and support her pursuits.

Before marriage, you can measure this by how he talks about your daughter and her interests. Does he make fun of her "hobbies," or brag about her expertise? On a given weekend, is he supportive of her interests, or does he subordinate them in favor of his own? Is he the sort of man who would be willing to give up Saturday golf to watch the children so his wife is able to attend an art class, for example?

A friend recently told me a story about an apple orchard purchased by a developer who intended to build a housing development on the property. Because of delays in the permitting, the orchard was ignored for a year. When harvest time arrived the following season, the fruit was smaller, much less plenteous, and less tasty than it had been the year before. Just one year of leaving the orchard untended resulted in significant deterioration.

Women who are cared for become more and more beautiful each year. You have been a farmer, if you will, and your daughter has developed into a beautiful and fruitful tree. You want to make sure that her new husband will be someone who will nurture and care for her so she will continue to grow in beauty and productivity.

Frederick Buechner states it well when he says, "the place God calls you to is the place where your deep gladness and the world's deep hunger meet."[3] You want a son-in-law who understands his call and supports your daughter in hers.

Bottom line:

- Does he have something he is really excited about in life?
- Are his passions in conflict with your daughter's passions, or will they mesh nicely?
- Have you observed your daughter grow more full of life and character since she has begun seeing him?

---

3. Buechner, F. (1973). *Wishful Thinking: A Theological ABC*, Harper & Row.

"What does scripture mean when it says, 'the husband is the head of the wife'?"

Answers you don't want to hear:

- Dude, like, it's like, I'm like, the *boss*.
- It means the little lady does what I say.
- My pastor said it doesn't apply today.
- I dunno, it meant nothing in my house.
- My parole officer said I was hard-headed. Is that what you're lookin' for?

Answers you do want to hear:

- To fully know what I am to be as a husband, I need to study scripture in order to learn how Christ interacted with the church.
- It means that I am responsible to God for my family's well-being.
- It means that I am to serve our family sacrificially.
- It means that true love is seen in service.
- It means I am to never use my position of authority in the home for my own ends.

Critical concepts you need to hear:

- He understands his responsibility before God to serve his family and put their needs ahead of his own.
- He understands that "head of the home" does not mean that he is the dictator.
- His motivation for marrying your daughter is so that he can meet her needs.

For those who want more:

Many men read "for the husband is the head of the wife..."[1] and then close the Bible, feeling "that's enough scripture for today." They then apply the concept of "head" as it is understood in the secular marketplace to "head" in the marital relationship. "That must mean I am in charge, like the owner of the company," they think. "Everyone else has to do what I say and serve me."

The Apostle Paul clarifies what he means by "head of the wife"—in case there might be any confusion—when he completes his sentence with "as Christ is the head of the church." First, this eliminates any confusion about whether or not husbands have authority in the marriage relationship. There is no confusion over whether Christ is the authority in the church. He is. Second, as "head of the church," Christ never used His authority for selfish ends. He always used his authority to serve. He always put the needs of others ahead of his own. Christ "did not come to be served, but to serve . . ."[2]

---

1. Ephesians 5:23
2. Mark 10:45

Many people today are very uncomfortable with the teaching that the husband has "authority over the wife," and prefer the phrase "responsibility for the wife." The reality is, however, that one cannot be responsible for something unless one also has authority over it. Many of us have at one time or another been given responsibility for something, and yet have not had the authority necessary to make anything happen. We know that such situations can be very frustrating. Responsibility without authority doesn't work.

With a husband's authority comes an immense amount of responsibility. It is interesting that in the Genesis account of the fall, Eve eats the fruit first—yet, throughout scripture, it is Adam who is held responsible for sin entering the world.[3] Scripture says that after Eve ate the fruit, she gave some to Adam, "who was with her."[4] Every indication is that Adam was there but was uninvolved, mentally absent, lights on but no one home.

What happened in the garden thousands of years ago is repeated daily in homes around the world. Men are home but uninvolved. One of the most common complaints from wives is that their husbands are absent, take no initiative, and seem uninterested in life at home.

Biblical leadership is doing what is right and beneficial to those you are leading, regardless of the cost to yourself. Daniel was a leader when he chose not to defile himself with the king's food and wine even though it could have cost him his position, or even his life.[5] Moses was a leader

---

3. Romans 5:12
4. Genesis 3:6
5. Daniel 1:1–20

GLASBERGEN

"You have a 30 year mortgage, a 5 year car lease, and a lifetime gym membership...but you're afraid of commitment?"

when he chose to identify himself with the Hebrews "rather than to enjoy the pleasures of sin for a short time."[6] For many husbands, leading means doing what is best for the family, regardless of what the guys at work may say. Leading may mean not accepting the promotion because it will hinder you in meeting your God-given responsibility to first lead at home. It may mean playing less golf so you can be present at home more of the time. It may mean that you spend more time reading God's word so you can set the tone at home.

The attributes of good leadership can be seen in many ways even while a man is still single. Does this young man insist on his own way? Does he expect to eat what he

---

6. Hebrews 11:24–26; see also Exodus 2:1–12

wants, where he wants, when he wants? Are the leisure activities he and your daughter participate in all his favorite activities? In their sexual relationship, did he show the leadership in standards of sexual purity, or did he push until your daughter said "stop"? Many young women will tell their dates they felt they went too far physically the night before, only to hear "But you never said 'stop.'" Such a statement reveals a man who will probably rely on his wife to be the moral and spiritual compass. He will likely play as much golf as he can get away with until she says "stop," or will work as long as he can until she calls him to come home. You want a man for your daughter who will lead, who will do the right thing on his own initiative, who will not abdicate all responsibility and put the burden on your daughter.

One final thought. Your daughter may say, "My boy-friend is a servant. He always says we can do whatever I want. When I ask, 'What are we going to do tonight?' or 'Where are we going?' he always says, 'Whatever you want, dear.'" Such words sound nice at first—and can be nice on occasion—but as a consistent refrain they indicate a man with little initiative, creativity, or leadership. He just made your daughter the leader, and for most women that gets old quickly.

Bottom line:

- Does he take his cues on how to lead from Christ's example to the church?

- Does he have a reputation as someone who puts others' needs ahead of his own?
- Does he understand the enormous responsibility of leadership he is about to undertake?

"What does it mean for you to love my daughter 'as Christ loved the church'?"

Answers you don't want to hear:

- I think love is different for each person.
- I don't really go to church.
- That's a good question . . . I dunno.
- Do it to others before they do it to you.
- My parole officer said I need religion.

Answers you do want to hear:

- It means that Christ is my example of what true love is, and I am to imitate Him as I care for my wife.
- It means I am to be willing to sacrifice my very life for her.
- It means that I am to serve her and put her needs before mine, as Christ did for the church.
- It means that I must use my position as "head of the wife" to serve my wife.
- It means that I should do all I can to care for her and put her needs ahead of my own.

Critical concepts you need to hear:

- That he does not see his position as one of authoritarian leadership.
- That he understands that Christ is the model for how he is to treat your daughter.
- That being "head of the wife" does not imply entitlement, but rather demands servanthood.

For those who want more:

What an impossible task this is—to love our wives as Christ loved the church—and yet that is exactly what scripture calls us to do.[1] You want the man who will marry your daughter to consider scripture his guide to understanding his role as a husband; more specifically, he should use Christ's love for the church as his example.

Loving our wives as Christ loved the church involves at least three things: servanthood, spiritual leadership, and helping our wives become more radiant.

Servanthood

Many men who understand scripture read this, grasp Christ's sacrifice of His life for the church, and confidently say, "I would be willing to give my life for my wife. If an eighteen-wheeler were coming at us, I would push my wife out of the way and give my life for her." That is a great—and safe—interpretation, since it will never happen. It is interesting how many men say they are willing to give their

---

1. Ephesians 5:25–30

very lives for their spouses, yet are not willing to skip any golf games, watch less television, or come home from work in time for dinner, even though their priorities have a negative effect on their marital and family life.

For too long, men have seen their wives as servants and themselves as kings. More accurately, what scripture says, if anything, is that the husband is not to be seen as the king of the castle but as the *servant* in the castle. Certainly husband and wife are to serve each other, but when push comes to shove, the husband is called on to be the chief servant.

A servant attitude, or its absence, can be detected prior to marriage. If the activities of the couple are always "his"

"Women want more these days, Bill—it's not enough just to be a jerk anymore."

activities, if the places they eat are always "his" places, or if the friends they hang out with are always "his" friends, then "Houston, we have a problem."

You want to see a man who has a track record of service, not selfishness, because your daughter is about to commit to a relationship of respect and submission to this man. Make sure he is a man who is known for sacrificial service instead of an attitude of entitlement. Your daughter is directed by scripture to submit to and respect her husband.[2] Make sure he is a man she is prepared to submit to and respect for the rest of her life. This side of the altar, the choice is hers.

Spiritual leadership

A common cry of wives today is that their husbands do not lead spiritually. For some reason, the women in this world do seem more naturally inclined to be Bible readers and to participate in group Bible studies. We men need to get going and start studying God's word. How can we love our wives as Christ loved the church if we don't know how Christ lived and loved?

Prayer in marriage is a powerful thing and thus a target of attack from the enemy. Husbands: *Lead* in prayer. She will "out-pray" you often in length and style, but don't give up. Couples who pray together regularly have a significantly reduced chance of divorce, according to our observation and experiences and the corroboration of other experts in the field. Alternate odd and even days as to who initiates prayer. Find a regular time that works for both of you. Pray.

---

2. Ephesians 5:22–23, 33

Helping her become more radiant

At every wedding I perform I look at the groom and say, "See how radiant your wife looks." I then say, "Thirty years from now your bride should look even more radiant because you have studied her and know her and have made it possible for her to develop her gifts, abilities, talents, and passions."

For too many years husbands have put their wives' interests on the shelf as they have pursued their own interests at great cost to their wives.

Bottom line:

- Have you observed him serving your daughter during their relationship and putting her interests and desires ahead of his own?
- Have you observed him being a student of scripture so he understands the example of Christ's love for "His bride"?
- Do you see him generally acting as a servant to others, or as one who expects others to serve him?

"How do you plan to provide for her financially?"

Answers you don't want to hear:

- I really haven't given that much thought.
- Your daughter said we could live with you.
- I'll be a "stay-at-home husband"; I don't plan to work.
- God will provide.
- My parole officer said he would line up work for me.

Answers you do want to hear:

- The job that I have had for a number of years is fulfilling and seems to be quite secure.
- I expect to find a job in my field as soon as I graduate in the spring. I have interned in the field and done well.
- I have a good savings account from jobs I have held over the years and have been on my own since college.
- I plan to continue in the ministry. I realize this is not the most lucrative vocation, but your daughter and I are willing to live simply, and I am committed to being the primary provider in our home.

- I have been learning the trade in my father's business for years and he plans to have me become a partner in the business as soon as I graduate.

Critical concepts you need to hear:

- He is industrious.
- He has a track record of a good work ethic.
- He has a clear direction for his future.

For those who want more:

We may have acted irritated when our daughter asked us for money, but deep down it felt good to know we were the provider for the family and were able to take care of her needs—and often her wants.

One of the difficult tasks a father has is to realize that when scripture says our daughters are to "leave home," it literally means to cut off, to sever, to abandon. Certainly this does not mean relationally, but it does mean that her allegiance and dependence are transferred from you, her father, to her new husband. One of the realities of this transfer is that her new husband may not be able to provide for her in the fashion to which she has become accustomed. It may be hard for us to see our daughter make do with less, but providing "on the sly" or even overtly so she will be "comfortable" is very emasculating for her husband. For this reason I believe couples should not marry until they are able to completely support themselves. Some well-intentioned parents pay for their children's ongoing education after they are married. I believe this is unwise and encourages an unhealthy dependence on the parents. This is certainly not to say that as parents you should not be free to give gifts to your married children, but they should not be in the form of loans or ongoing "gifts" that keep your children tied to you, dependent on you, or obligated in any way.

One of the ways to help lessen the temptation to "help out" is to make sure your daughter is marrying someone who is able to provide for her.

Again, looking at past performance is more helpful than listening to promises for the future. I have counseled too many couples in which the woman is supporting the family even though her husband, who had never held a steady job,

"I think I can make you very happy if I can get funded."

promised to find work—*after* they were married.

Perhaps you have given your daughter every material thing she ever wanted: she has worn designer clothes, driven new cars, and traveled extensively—but never had you around. Many girls with driven, non-involved dads are susceptible to marrying a man who may not have much drive or financial resources, but has *time* for her. Too often a young lady wakes up a few years into her marriage and realizes that the reason her boyfriend always had time for her was because he didn't *do* anything. If you have been a workaholic, absent dad, ask forgiveness from your daughter before you give the lecture, "How will he ever provide for you?"

Some young men are just graduating from college or graduate school and have pretty much devoted themselves to their academic pursuits. If this is the case, look for someone who has initiative, a good work ethic, confidence, integrity, and a clear direction for life. It is not a bad thing, however, for a couple to wait a year after he is out of college to get himself established and on his own before he becomes the primary provider for your daughter.

Be wary of the man who has no money, no job, and no direction in life. As I have said to my daughters, "no money, no honey."

Bottom line:

- Does he work? How long has he worked?
- Does he have savings?
- Does he have a plan for his life?

"How are you honoring my daughter sexually, and how will you honor her after marriage?"

Answers you don't want to hear:

- Yes, she says I'm a great sexual partner.
- I always stop when she says she really means it.
- Do you honestly believe any one woman can sexually satisfy a man for life?
- It's not really clear what the word "fornicate" means in the original Greek.
- My parole officer said "Your honor" during my sexual offense hearing.

Answers you do want to hear:

- I am thankful that though we struggle with sexual desire, we have not done anything we are embarrassed about or ashamed of.
- We have attempted to follow the teaching we received not to sexually arouse one another until we are married.[1]

1. Song of Solomon 2:7, 3:5, 8:4

- We have not always held to our boundaries, but we are thankful for forgiveness and have made a commitment to stay sexually pure until marriage.
- Before committing my life to Christ, I did not treat women as I should have. I am determined not to make that mistake with your daughter.
- My goal as a married man is not to receive sexual pleasure from anything or anyone other than my wife.

Critical concepts you need to hear:

- His commitment to scriptural guidelines on physical involvement supersedes his "hormonal urges."
- He is committed to leading in this area of their relationship.
- He is able to exhibit self-control instead of expecting instant gratification when it comes to sexual expression.

For those who want more:

God's gift of the sexual relationship between husband and wife is designed for intimacy, unity, and relational one-ness. Satan loves to take what God intended to bring joy to his children and glory to Himself, and persuade us to use it outside of God's design. The sexual relationship in marriage is designed to be so satisfying, unifying, erotic, and passion-ate that it in essence elevates the married couple above their day-to-day problems. In the passion of oneness they forget their problems and revel in the intimacy they have always longed for. For a brief time they are "blinded" from their problems because of the delight of their sexual intimacy.

In the same way the physical act of sexual intimacy can easily "blind" an unmarried couple to those things which will likely challenge them after marriage.

Sex "feels" like intimacy but is not necessarily so. That is why scripture's sequence of leaving, cleaving, and then becoming one is so important. The lifelong decision for marriage should be made *before* the "blinding" experience of sexual intimacy. Sex is an expression of marital intimacy, but not a means to marital commitment.

It is critical that couples enter into marriage with as much objectivity as possible. Our culture today has largely separated sexual expression from a committed relationship and made it an activity for immediate gratification devoid of relational commitment. Many young couples come to my wife Virginia and me for counseling and talk about the sexual dysfunction they are experiencing. When we ask them about their sexual involvement before marriage, most admit they were sexually involved and satisfied, and are surprised and dismayed that they are not experiencing sexual satisfaction within marriage. There are a variety of reasons for this. Some suffer from guilt over their sexual sin outside of marriage; many have never confessed and repented of their sin. Often a woman admits that she allowed herself to become sexually involved before marriage because she was afraid that if she didn't, she would lose her boyfriend—and now that she is married, she feels no need to continue to please his every fantasy and desire. For others, both men and women, the illicit nature of premarital sex was simply more tantalizing than marital sex.

In this age, when many have had a variety of partners and experiences apart from marriage, couples wonder why marital sex is not as thrilling. Marital sexual expression is designed to be an absolutely wonderful, intimate, and erotic experience. It is difficult, however, for marital sex to compete with illicit sex. Think of it: you experience sex with multiple partners who, so it seems, will do virtually anything you wish, and then you marry and are expected to have a sexual relationship with only one person and do only those things your spouse is comfortable with.

The sexual relationship was designed by God to bring couples closer relationally. When the sexual experience prior to marriage is largely focused on meeting a sexual urge or getting a new sexual high, one expects sex within marriage to be that way as well, and views sex primarily as a way to achieve a sexual thrill rather than an intimate experience.

You want to know if the man who is asking to marry your daughter has controlled his sexual urges not only with your daughter, but also with other women in earlier relationships. Is he bringing any sexually transmitted diseases into the relationship? In cases where the young man may have been involved in relationships outside of God's design for purity, it is important to see a subsequent track record of sexual purity, a medical report clearing him from sexually transmitted diseases, and a repentant, humble spirit.

Many couples feel that marriage will solve the sexual frustration and temptations they are experiencing prior to marriage. The reality is that if a man is sexually demanding prior to marriage, he will likely be sexually demanding after marriage. You want a man who will honor your daughter and respect her sexually not only before marriage, but within marriage as well.

Has he been involved at all with sexually explicit material? What are his habits when it comes to books, magazines, movies, and television—and what is their effect on his sexual appetite? Sexual addiction and involvements have destroyed far too many marriages for you to be unconcerned. Again, you want a track record of purity, not a promise to change.

As much as we would like for our daughters to marry someone who has remained sexually pure, the statistics are not in our favor. The great news of the gospel is that although all of us—certainly dads included—have fallen short of God's

"You'd better ask your grandparents about that, son—my generation is very uncomfortable talking about abstinence."

best, He has made a way for us to be forgiven and restored. It is critical, both theologically and experientially, for us to believe that in Christ we do become a new creation. God is in the business of forgiveness and new starts. We must not "write off" our daughters or prospective son-in-laws because of sins confessed and forgiven.

I want my daughter to marry someone who honors her sexually and sees sexual purity as a higher value than instant gratification. I want for her the least amount of obstacles to a healthy, vibrant, satisfying sexual relationship in marriage.

Bottom line:

- Has he exhibited self-control in the area of sexual purity?
- Does he understand the role of sexual expression as relational in nature?
- Does he understand that women need relational closeness to enter into sexual expression, or does he see sexual involvement as her duty and his right?

Question 8

"How will you encourage my daughter to grow spiritually?"

Answers you don't want to hear:

- What exactly do you mean by "spiritual"?
- Hate to tell you, Pops, but your daughter is *so* over religion.
- I'm really not into that spiritual stuff.
- There are many roads to spiritual enlightenment.
- My parole officer said I should marry a spiritual person.

Answers you do want to hear:

- We talk about the Lord as a routine part of our conversations.
- I tell her what God is teaching me in my personal study and ask about what she is learning from God.
- I believe meeting with other believers regularly in church is critical to our spiritual growth.
- We both believe in prayer, but currently do not spend a lot of time together in prayer, because we have

63

found it to be quite an intimate experience.

We pray when we have decisions to make, and I plan to make prayer together a central part of each day after we are married.

Critical concepts you need to hear:

- He is growing spiritually.
- He sees spiritual vitality as central to their relationship.
- Your daughter is growing spiritually because of who he is and his encouragement and challenge to her.

For those who want more:

You want to hear first that he has a vital personal commitment to Christ and a desire to continue to grow in his own spiritual disciplines. Jack and Cynthia Heald have said that they feel a man walking closely with his Lord will be a man rightly related to his wife, and a wife walking closely with her Lord will be a woman rightly related to her husband.[1] It is only in God's word that we understand how we are to treat each other as husband and wife. "Husbands, love your wives, just as Christ loved the church . . ."[2] You want your daughter to be married to a man who knows and loves scripture well enough to understand how Christ loved

---

1. Heald, J., and Heald, C. (2000). *Walking Together: Building a Marriage in a Fallen World.* Colorado Springs, CO: NavPress Publishing Group.
2. Ephesians 5:25

the church and how to apply this understanding to the marriage relationship.

You want to hear him express how he sees the spiritual aspects of his relationship with your daughter as central to their experience. Many women marry men who profess to be believers but have no vibrancy in their relationship with Christ. A man called to lead your daughter spiritually should have a vibrant faith, not just a "Sure, I believe" faith.

Make sure his faith experience is independent of any desire to please your daughter. Ideally, he will participate in Bible studies with other men. When your daughter is sick or traveling and not able to attend church, you want to observe him pursuing his spiritual life anyway, not because of his relationship with your daughter, but because of his relationship with Christ.

"I'm going to Europe to find myself, and John is going to Asia to find himself."

Look for a man who takes initiative in spiritual matters. He should not take his lead from your daughter, but lead her into a more vibrant walk with Christ. Part of Paul's admonition to husbands is to wash their wives in God's word. Certainly this means that the husband of your daughter must take seriously his need to know the Bible and encourage his wife in God's ways.

You want to see your daughter growing closer to the Lord as a result of their experiences together. This would include—but not be limited to—church involvement, and would extend to books being read, conferences attended, and music listened to.

You want to see them both growing closer to the Lord because of their lives together, challenging and encouraging each other to more fully reflect the image of God.

Bottom line:

- Is he growing in his personal walk with Jesus?
- Is your daughter closer to the Lord because of her relationship with him?
- Do you believe he will lead their home in a way that is pleasing to the Lord?

"What are the absolutes that drive your decisions?"

Answers you don't want to hear:

- Listen, old man, absolutes are so *yesterday*.
- What is right to one person is wrong to another, so who really knows?
- I try to let life just happen and go with the flow. You know what I mean?
- I don't think anyone should make decisions for another person.
- My parole officer said I absolutely better not drive drunk any more, or someone else would be making all my decisions.

Answers you do want to hear:

- I believe that God's word should ultimately drive all my decisions.
- I believe my decisions should be made according to what is morally right.
- I do not pursue anything illegal, immoral, or unethical.

- I try to seek counsel from wise men and women who really understand God's word.
- I believe God has given us each a conscience and if that leading does not contradict God's word, I go with that.

Critical concepts you need to hear:

- God's word is the final authority on all issues.
- He surrounds himself with those who are older and wiser to make decisions.
- He believes in absolutes regarding those things that are legal, moral, and ethical.

For those who want more:

Years ago I was the director of a seaside camp on a desert island. I was giving a tour to a very wealthy man who observed that we had an accumulation of old refrigerators in our maintenance yard that were unsightly. He asked why we didn't dispose of them. I explained to him that we were saving them until we had enough to ship off the island at a more reasonable cost than shipping them one at a time. He asked me why we didn't just take them out in the ocean and dump them. I replied that that was illegal, to which he said, "*At night?*"

Look for a man who believes in submitting to authority, even at night!

Look for a man who believes in absolutes. He sees

Marry me, Judith . . . with the understanding, of course,
that past performance is not a guarantee of future results.

God's word as his final authority on all issues. He is not
guided merely by what *feels* right, nor by what our culture
approves, nor by his own "conscience."

When it comes to financial decisions, I want my daughter
to marry a man who does what is legal, without hesitation,
instead of figuring what he can get away with. When he
gives his word, I want him to keep his word—even if "chang-
ing his mind" might be more lucrative or fun. In the area of
relationships, I want to know that the authority of scripture
is more important than responding to his raging hormones.
In the area of family, I want a son-in-law who honors scripture over family or ethnic tradition. In the area of language,
I want a son-in-law who seeks to follow the command of

God's word to "Let no unwholesome talk come out of your mouth"[1] rather than to let his words fly because he "needs to get it out."

In all these areas, I am describing a man who holds God's word as his final authority—even when it goes against his feelings, his desire for fun, or his financial gain.

I know a young man who reported to the IRS all the tips he received at his job as a waiter even though it infuriated his fellow waiters, who reported only "traceable" wages, not including tips. He did it because scripture tells us not to steal or lie. Eventually it cost him his job, but he left with a clear conscience.

Joseph of the Old Testament was a man who trusted God and was obedient to him instead of giving in to Potiphar's wife. He obeyed first and asked questions later. Even when thrown in jail unfairly, he honored God instead of retaliating with ungodly behavior.[2] I want such a husband for each of my daughters. I trust you want no less for yours.

Bottom line:

- Is he willing to trust God to take care of him even when a "shady deal" would be more lucrative?
- Does He see God's word as absolutely trustworthy in its entirety?
- Is he willing to follow God's word, even if it might mean suffering hardship or persecution?

---

1. Ephesians 4:29
2. Genesis 39:1–20

"What if marriage doesn't turn out to be what you imagined?"

Answers you don't want to hear:

- "Bail out before you crash" is what I've always said.
- I'd see it as a learning experience—after all, I *do* deserve to be happy.
- Marriage is like a computer—it's always good to upgrade.
- My uncle says, "There are always more fish in the sea."
- My parole officer says, "You got to know when to hold them and know when to fold them."

Answers you do want to hear:

- My commitment is to your daughter, not to a dream.
- If it is not what I had imagined, I would need to examine whether my expectations were Biblical and realistic.
- I guess I would need to look at myself first and see how I might be contributing to the difficulties we are having.
- I would pray and ask God to reveal to both of us what we need to do to have a more God-honoring marriage.

- I trust that by having regular "marital check-ups" through marriage seminars and retreats, we could quickly address our issues.

Critical concepts you need to hear:

- He sees the marriage as a lifelong covenant, not a negotiable contract.
- He will seek help quickly if the marriage is not going well.
- He will consider whether some of his expectations about marriage were unrealistic.

For those who want more:

Statistically speaking, approximately half of those who marry will divorce at one time or another. It has been suggested that of those who do not divorce, only a small percentage would consider themselves happily married. With those sobering thoughts, we launch into the last question: "What are you going to do if it does not go as planned?"

The first thing you want to know is that this young man has an "until death do us part" mentality going into marriage. Far too many couples entering marriage have an "until we are not happy" mentality or "until it doesn't go as I thought it would" mentality. You can often get a hint from how he talks about other marriages that did not last. If the tenor of his comments leans toward "They just weren't happy" or "You can't blame them for breaking up, since he found someone who really was better suited" or "I guess she just didn't realize how much he would travel," it reveals a man who may give up easily or have a low view of covenant.

You also are able to view how he has responded in other relationships when they did not go according to his plan. Was he comfortable with breaking commitments to others when the going got tough?

You want to see a man who is willing to search himself for areas in which he could improve, which would in turn improve his marriage. He should not be one who excuses his actions because of someone else. He should not try to blame your daughter for any tension they may have.

You want to see a man who does not, at the first sign of dissatisfaction, start looking around to see what other options there might be. He works on what he has rather than coveting what he does not have. He does not threaten

"You take all the time you need, Larry—this certainly is a big decision."

to leave the relationship every time they have an argument. He is able to say he was wrong and to ask forgiveness.

She too!

Bottom line:

- He sees marriage as a work in progress.
- He is able to view himself realistically and take responsibility for his actions.
- He plans to grow old with your daughter, no matter how challenging life may become.

Questions Dads Ask

But what if I have not been involved in my daughter's life?

I love the saying "It is never too late to start doing the right thing." I doubt there is a dad who would say, "I don't love my daughter," but all of us would say, "I have not always shown her my love in ways she really understood." No matter where your relationship is with your daughter, we serve a God who loves to be involved in making reconciliation happen.

Here are a few thoughts.

An apology is always the best place to start. Apologize for traveling so much, for being so harsh, for not going to her events, for leaving her mom, or for being focused on your own interests ahead of the family's. These are just examples. You know what your list is.

Make sure you apologize without any "buts." "I am sorry I was so harsh, but if you had been obedient . . ." Anything uttered after the "but" cancels out the apology. It attempts to release you from responsibility for your actions and put the blame on someone else, in this case your daughter.

Second, express your desire to be more of the dad you always should have been. Acknowledge that though you can't "make up" for who you were, you want very much to establish a relationship now as an adult.

Third, give your daughter permission to express to you the ways she has felt hurt by you or neglected by you. It is extremely important at this time that you simply listen to your daughter and not respond defensively, even if you don't agree with all her assessments. Acceptable responses would be something like "I am sorry you were affected in that way" or "I am sorry you were hurt so deeply" or "I never wanted to hurt you and I am so sorry my actions or lack thereof have hurt you."

Fourth, in the days, weeks, and months that follow, take the initiative to write, to call, and to go out together. Even if she is less than enthusiastic, make the effort so she knows you sincerely care.

Finally, pray regularly that the Lord will replace "what the locust has eaten." Pray for your daughter's physical, emotional, relational, and spiritual health.

For some dads, the written word seems to work better as an initial communication. A letter has a number of things going for it. It can be revised and polished to say exactly what you want it to say. It will not be interrupted and perhaps sidetracked into a volatile exchange. It gives your daughter something to refer back to as she contemplates your desired relationship with her.

Whatever your form of communication, you want your daughter to know you love her and desire to be more fully a part of her life.

What if I have no peace about this relationship?

There are two categories of dads with this question: those who have had little relationship with their daughters and no peace, and those who have a close relationship with their daughters and no peace.

For those who have had little relationship with their daughters:

Perhaps the first thing you need to do is apologize to your daughter for not being the dad you should have been. Tell her that you are aware that it seems a bit odd now that at this point in life you have all sorts of advice and want to become close.

You may need to express that although you have not always been there for her, or not been consistent, or not lived a life worth imitating . . . (fill in the blank), you want her to know you do love her and want the very best for her. Tell her you realize your counsel may seem hollow at this time, but you deeply want for her a man who will cherish her, provide for her, and lead her in God's ways.

Often we need to realize that years ago we forfeited the "right" to be the voice giving "life choices" advice. If this is so, encourage your daughter and her prospective husband to seek others who are more objective and can help them process this critical decision in life.

Make sure the concerns you share are substantive concerns—those that are driven by moral or Biblical positions and not simply personal preferences. For instance, a less than helpful concern would be "His hair is too long" or "He doesn't dress well" or "His profession will never give you the lifestyle I gave you." Make sure that the concerns you express have to do with convictions and character.

If you are a believer in Christ, pray that God will give you His wisdom and grace to speak into her life in a way she will hear, or provide someone else who will be able to do this.

For those who have a close relationship with their daughters:

This situation is especially difficult because you have most likely seen your daughter make pretty decent decisions and now a big one comes and she seems to be blowing it.

Our first inclination is to react strongly, saying things like "You can't marry him" or "If you marry him I will be so disappointed in you" or "We have not raised you to marry someone like this."

Ideally you would be having some ongoing discussions long before "the question" is popped. Many times we fail in one of two ways. We either say nothing and hope for the best, or we overreact and drive her into his arms.

Having early, open-ended discussions tends to be most productive. Even after engagement, the goal is to keep listening and talking so they are able to verbalize their thoughts with you. Being as positive as you are able as you start the discussion usually helps. "He sure is talented on that guitar" may be a more beneficial leading sentence than "He's crazy to think he will ever make a living playing guitar."

Asking questions that give your daughter the opportunity to say why she wants to marry him may be more productive than you starting off by telling her why she shouldn't marry him.

When she says, "Because he loves me" or "Because he is so fun" you should not say, "And you expect to live on love?" or "You won't be laughing when you have no food to eat." Instead, after listening to why she loves him or what she sees as his strengths, ask her what her biggest concerns are about their relationship or what concerns she has about marrying him. If she hits on one you agree with, don't say "*Bingo*, now you're talking some sense!" Instead say, "Yes, I actually have wondered about that myself" or "It will be important to see how he develops in this area before making a life-long commitment."

If the concern is in the area of his profession or his ability to provide for your daughter, you may express that as, "This certainly isn't a moral issue, but it could become a significant area of challenge for your marriage."

If the reason for your hesitation has to do with a Biblical or moral issue, you can enter the conversation by saying something like, "Frankly, I am a bit surprised with your thinking since you have always seemed to agree with scripture about only marrying a Christian."

If you believe the marriage will be sinful—a Christian marrying a non-Christian (see 2 Corinthians 6:14)—you have every reason to say something like "Because your choice to marry someone who does not share your relationship with Christ is directly in opposition to the teaching of scripture, I am afraid I cannot give my blessing on your marriage. This is very hurtful to me and I am sure to you, since I always expected the preparation for marriage to be such a joyous time. I will always love you and pray for God's best for you, but I cannot go against God's clear teaching on this one. I am not saying I will not be at the wedding nor be cordial, but I cannot support what I believe will be in direct disobedience to scripture."

One of the issues that may arise is the finances for the wedding. My suggestion would be that you allocate an amount you feel is appropriate for the wedding and give it to her. (The loving father of the prodigal gave the younger son his inheritance, even though he was sure he would squander it.[1]) Don't use money as leverage to force her choices in line with your wishes.

In the end, you want to pray that God will touch her heart and guide her. You want to do all that is in your power to maintain relationships. You always want to have the door open so that you are able to have a relationship that, prayerfully, will someday lead to the marriage you had always envisioned for your daughter. You want her to know that whether or not her choices match your wishes, you will always love her.

In the end, you want to be a man who speaks truth and grace, from His word. Truth and grace will serve you well.

May God give you His wisdom and love.

---

1. Read this story in Luke 15:11–32.

What guy is going to pass this test?

Or,
"If I had had to answer these questions, I'd still be single."

What is a "passing grade"? 6 out of 10? 8 out of 10? 10 out of 10? This is not a test, of course, but an interview. After an interview, the interviewer sits back and makes his decision—not based on arithmetic, but on a "gut response," an "intuitive observation," or a "calculated risk." There are no perfect young men out there—and if we are honest, we'll admit that even our daughters are not perfect. Even so, the goal is to have your daughter marry a man who has character and convictions that you believe he will continue to develop in a positive direction.

It is tempting for us as fathers to judge the 20-something-year-old against the standard of our 50-year-old maturity and status in life. When a pitcher is selected for the minors, he is chosen on the basis of his past performance and his potential success, not on whether he is able to perform in the majors at that time. Marriage, even in the best of cases, is an act of faith. We can't guarantee success, but we are able to discern and observe patterns that we believe will come to fruition.

What about grace and God's power to change the direction of a young man's life? Naturally, we would love for our daughter to marry a man with as little baggage as possible, but even more important is for her to marry a man who understands God's grace in his life. Make sure he has a track record long enough that you can see whether his true heart and character have changed and that he has not simply modified his behavior for the time being.

Hopefully, the moment of his "seeking permission" will not be the first time you have thought of these questions or discussed them with your daughter and her boyfriend. We fathers have an obligation to get to know the men in our daughters' lives as much as possible. The proposal of marriage should never come as a shock to your daughter, and the answers to these questions should not be a shock to the dad on the night his daughter's suitor asks for her hand in marriage.

Hey, in the end, your daughter will make the decision on who she will marry. You want to do all you can, as soon as you can, to enter into a discussion and not simply issue an edict. Your desire, if they get married, is for them to continue to have an ear to learn from your wisdom, *when they ask*.

Will anyone ever be good enough for your little girl? I doubt it. But then again, look at the man your father-in-law allowed to marry *his* daughter.

What if I'm a young dad just starting to parent?

Top 10 Tips on Parenting

There certainly are no guarantees in parenting, but there are probabilities. One of our greatest responsibilities as parents is to create the atmosphere most conducive to our children making God-honoring choices in life.

I am not an expert in parenting—I have only raised three daughters—but I am happy to pass on to you a few tips I have been taught along this path of parenthood, and specifically regarding being a father to my girls.

1. Model the sort of man you want them some day to be attracted to. One of the greatest compliments a father can receive is "Dad, how will I ever find a husband as great as you? You have set the bar mighty high."

2. Be authentic. Our children don't need to see perfect parents, but they do need to see authentic parents. They need to see parents who are willing to admit their mistakes, without blaming the children (not "I am sorry I yelled at you, but if you had done what I asked I wouldn't have" but "I am sorry I yelled at you," period).

3. Let them see your genuine love for the Lord and His word. It gives our children great security to know that our desire is to live our lives according to what God has clearly said is best, rather than how our emotions, hormones, or outside pressures dictate on any given day.

4. Don't be afraid to be the parent. They need you to be the gatekeeper, to protect them from those things that might be harmful to them—media, friends, activities, etc. You are called to be their parent before you are their friend.

5. Keep talking to them. Open communication starts when they are young. If you welcome their conversations at four, you are much more apt to have them talking to you when they are fourteen.

6. Expose them to people, events, and activities that will help them have a passion for growing up to be a person who loves Christ, His people, and those He cares about. Let them look forward to growing into an adult Christian. Don't forget to have fun. Christ came to give us life "to the full." Let them see that in you.

7. Give them time. There may be no other item that spells love to our children more clearly than time. Be at their games, recitals, plays, and parent conferences. Put their activities on your schedule first and then fit your other commitments around them. I am convinced that many young women are drawn to boyfriends without drive, vision, or passion because these women were raised by absent dads. Such boyfriends not only have

time for them, but offer affirmation and affection—and dad was too busy for that. Always pursue relationship with them. Show them you care for them, and that you are interested in their worlds. Rules without relationship produce rebellion.

8. Love their mom. For the two-parent family there is no greater gift you can give to your children than a secure and loving home. They need to see what a vital marriage is like.

9. Love them unconditionally. This does not mean love all their actions and never discipline them, but do let them know that your love for them is not built on their performance or life choices. There is nothing they can do that will make you love them more or that will make you love them less.

10. Pray for them daily. There is a battle going on for their lives, and prayer is the weapon that is more powerful than any human program or technique. Pray that God will surround them with those who love Him and encourage them in His ways.

A Few Comments Specifically to Future Sons-in-law

The daunting tasks of asking and letting go

Asking for permission to marry a man's daughter, or even to date her, is a daunting task. It should not be done lightly. I remember putting my arm around a young man taking one of our daughters to the Junior/Senior prom and saying, "We have cared for our daughter for 17 years without anything bad happening to her. Don't do anything stupid that will mar that record in the next six hours. Understood?"

Parenting is by far the most exhausting job a man will ever have. A dad often feels inadequate to give his children the direction and wisdom they need. He often wishes he could go to school and on dates with them to protect them from poor choices. And then one day his daughter tells him she has found someone with whom she would like to spend the rest of her life, and it is not him.

This is the message I have for *every* prospective son-in-law: When our girls got in trouble as youngsters, I could rescue them. If they were at a party and it got out of hand, I could go and retrieve them. If they crashed the car, I could assure them things could be replaced. When you marry my daughter, nothing will change my love for her, nor my desire for the best for her, nor even my desire to protect her—but she will no longer be my responsibility, but yours. Perhaps that is why this is such a big deal to me. I will still have the emotional connection, but not the authority to do anything if my daughter is hurting.

From the day of your wedding forward, when the two of you want advice, I will always welcome the opportunity for conversation. But if my daughter calls me to get advice on how to relate with you, I will encourage her to seek help elsewhere. Not that I don't care, but I am no longer the one to be in alliance with her. You are now the one from whom and with whom she should seek advice. If the issue is you, she needs to seek other wise counsel, so her allegiance does not return to someone she has been called to leave in order to cleave to you.

Remember that scripture directs only children, not adults, to obey their parents.[1] As adults, you are to obey God. But scripture directs children and adults alike to *honor* their parents.[2] There may be times when you do not like how your wife's parents involve themselves in your lives. It is her role to deal with them. She may call them jerks, but you had better not. They are still her parents and she will still love them as such and will want their approval.

You may be called on to make family visits from time to time. I hope and pray you will have in-laws you enjoy. If you find them annoying, remember that is no reason to refuse to visit or to act like a bore while you are there. Suck it up and be an adult for the visit. Do it out of love for your wife.

---

1. Colossians 3:20
2. Exodus 20:12

Now, regarding *your* parents.   Scripture tells sons to leave because mama often won't let go.   Make sure your wife knows she is the number one woman in your life now. If there are areas in which she is insecure around your mom, protect her.   Always be an advocate for your wife.   Your mom may want to comment on how to cook for you, care for you, or raise your children.   It is not her place to coach you or your wife without your invitation.

Finally, remember that you are not getting grafted into a family tree; you and your wife are a new sapling starting your own life together.   As you both are secure in your love for each other, you will be able to return to your parents in an adult-to-adult relationship that is best for all.

Scripture says, "the two will become one . . . they are no longer two."[3]   All your decisions should now go through the grid: "Will this strengthen or hinder our relationship as husband and wife?"

When you propose marriage, be prepared to answer questions a dad might ask.   In the end, I think what *every* father wants to know is that his daughter will be loved, cherished, provided for, led in ways consistent with his faith position, and cared for in a way that allows her to flourish as a wife, mom, and individual.

May God give you incredible wisdom as you enter into this relationship of service that reflects most closely Christ's love for the church.   May you both find incredible joy as you honor the Lord in your marriage and honor each other.

---

3. Matthew 19:3–6

How do you propose to the woman you love?

Even though it was over 32 years ago, I remember it as if it were yesterday. Well, okay . . . I still *remember* it. Virginia had just finished finals for the fall semester. The date was December 15, 1975. The place was Coronado Beach, California. It was a beach we had walked on together many times before, but tonight was different. We had just finished a wonderful meal at Tom Ham's Lighthouse, and were now taking the memorable stroll.

As we started our walk, I offered her a Certs®. This should have been a clue, since you should never offer your date a breath mint. But this had nothing to do with Virginia's breath, and everything to do with a decision I had made not to kiss the girl I was dating until I asked her to marry me.

After the Certs®, I told Virginia I loved her and asked her if she would marry me and spend the rest of her life with me. She answered, "I need to think about that . . . *yes!*" And we kissed. Boy, did we kiss!

We then headed to her folks' house to ask her dad for her hand in marriage. Okay, so I got it backwards. (Upon hearing this story, my daughters said, *"Dad,* what was *wrong* with you? You are supposed to ask the father *before* asking the girl!") Anyway, we wrote down my financial assets (which didn't take long), figuring her dad would want to know how I was going to provide for his daughter.

Somehow I passed his questioning, and the rest—as they say—is history.

Gabe did a great job of proposing to my daughter Kari. Though there is no "script" for marriage proposals, let me describe how he did it, as well as give you a few principles that I believe apply across the board.

Gabe called me and set up a time to talk. Good start. He was respectful of my schedule by allowing me to set the time for a phone conversation. Face to face is recommended if possible, but in this case it was not.

So Gabe called me at the appointed time, and after our conversation—which lasted about a half hour as I asked him question after question—I gave my blessing. He then explained to me his plan for proposing to Kari.

Kari was with our family for a week at Campus By the Sea (CBS), the camp where our girls have spent their summers from the time they were born. As they grew older, the girls each served on our camp staff. There is no place on earth that means more to Kari than CBS. Gabe had been there once before. It was certainly not a place of significance to him. He had told Kari he couldn't join her for the week because of work. (Yes, he lied, but lying is permissible for surprises that include engagements.) He arranged with us to sneak him into camp while Kari was eating dinner. He then went up to the cross on the hill overlooking camp—a place of great meaning—and stayed there until Christina, a mentor friend of Kari's, "spontane-ously" asked her to take a walk with her to the cross after dinner. As soon as she delivered Kari to the cross and Kari saw Gabe, Christina vanished. Lisa, our middle daughter, positioned herself half way up the trail to the cross and told other campers wishing to hike to the cross that "the cross is closed." After Gabe proposed and Kari accepted, they came down into camp to the celebration of family and friends. It was a joyful and memorable evening!

Here are my tips for getting engaged. I have no Bible verses to back them up, but I believe the principles are important.

- Ask the girl's parents, father, or mother (if she has a single parent) for their blessing on your desire to marry their daughter—*before* you propose.
- Make sure the girl is likely to say yes. Proposals should be a surprise in timing, but not in fact. If the girl is shocked, you have not done your homework by taking time to develop the relationship.
- Remember, it is about her, not you. Know her prefer-ences. Know what place would be special to her and what type of proposal she would like. CBS meant noth-ing to Gabe. His friends and family were not there, but it was a special place to Kari, and her family and friends were close by.
- Don't buy the final ring unless you know her and her tastes. It is a real bummer to spend over a thousand dollars only to hear her say, "It's really nice . . . Did they have it in white gold?"
- Think about how she would like the world to know.

An introverted woman may not enjoy coming back from this romantic time to a house full of your favorite friends yelling congratulations. That means they knew before she did.

• Think it through. You may get only one shot at this. It is best to know what you are going to say, so she doesn't need to ask you, "Does this mean you want to marry me?"

• The day is both sacred and fun. Enjoy it fully. Remember that your proposal to her is a great time to show your future wife how much you know her, love her, and desire to put her interests and desires ahead of yours.

Other books and study guides
authored or co-authored by Paul A. Friesen
and available from Home Improvement Ministries:

Restoring the Fallen, InterVarsity Press
Letters to My Daughters, Home Improvement Ministries
Recapturing Eden, Home Improvement Ministries
Engagement Matters, Home Improvement Ministries

About the Author

Paul Friesen has been married for 31 years to his wife, Virginia, and they are the parents of three wonderful young women: Kari, Lisa, and Julie. Kari was married to Gabriel Garcia in February 2007. Paul and Virginia are the founders of Home Improvement Ministries (www.HIMweb.org), a non-profit organization dedicated to equipping individuals and churches to better encourage marriages and families in living out God's design for healthy relationships.

Paul writes, teaches, and counsels. He and Virginia regularly speak together at marriage, men's, and women's conferences across the country, as well as at family and parenting seminars, and have an ongoing ministry with several professional athletic teams. Paul and Virginia are (along with four others) co-authors of the book *Restoring the Fallen*, published by InterVarsity Press. In 2006, Home Improvement Ministries published Paul's book *Letters to My Daughters*, a series of letters he wrote to his three girls regarding the second most important decision in life: marriage.

Each summer, the Friesens travel to California to serve as program directors for InterVarsity Christian Fellowship's Campus by the Sea family camp programs. Their daughters have joined them there each year to serve alongside their parents.

Paul has a doctorate in Marriage and Family Therapy and a master's degree in Family Ministry, both from Gordon-Conwell Theological Seminary. Before founding Home Improvement Ministries in 2003, he was on staff at Grace Chapel in Lexington, Massachusetts, where he served as the Director of Men's and Family Ministries.

Paul and Virginia's greatest joy in life is knowing that their children are "walking in the truth."